Motorbikes

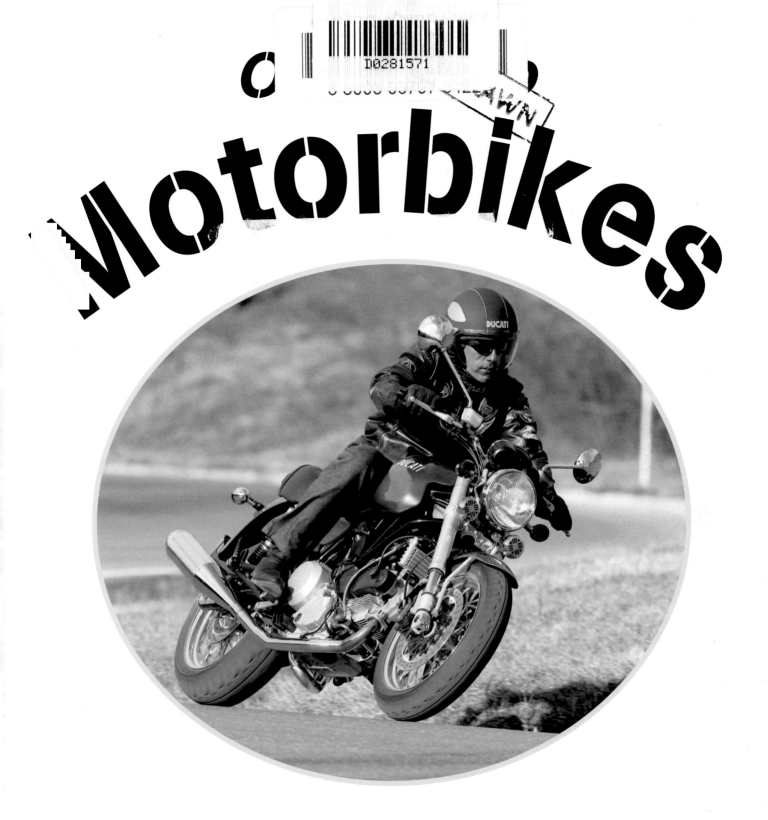

David and Penny Glover

WAYLAND

First published in 2007 by Wayland

Copyright © Wayland 2007
This paperback edition published in 2010 by Wayland

Wayland
338 Euston Road
London NW1 3BH

Wayland
Level 17/207 Kent Street
Sydney, NSW 2000

Editor: Camilla Lloyd
Editorial Assistant: Katie Powell
Designer: Elaine Wilkinson
Picture Researcher: Kathy Lockley

Picture Acknowledgements: The author and publisher would like to thank the following for allowing these pictures to be reproduced in this publication: Cover: Ducati (both); Bubbles Photolibrary/Alamy: 8, Lourens Smak/Alamy: 9, TNTMagazine/Alamy: 11b, Joern Sackermann/ Alamy: 14, Mike Greenslade/Alamy: 15, Martin Jenkinson/Alamy: 19, Colin Woodbridge/Alamy: 21; Patrick Bennett/Corbis: 7, Torlief Svenson/ Corbis: 2, 10, Gene Blevins/LA Daily News/Corbis: 11t, Alain Nognes/ Corbis: 12, Reuters/Corbis: 13, Matthias Hiekel/epa/Corbis: 20t, Pascal Rossignol/Reuters/Corbis: 20b; Ducati: 1, 4, 18; Kawaski: 6; Popperfoto. com: 22; Rex Features: 16t, 17; Nigel Dickenson/Still Pictures: 5; Suzuki: 16b.

With special thanks to Ducati, Kawasaki and Suzuki.

British Library Cataloguing in Publication Data
Glover, David, 1953 Sept. 4-
        Motorbikes. - (On the go)
        1. Motorcycles - Juvenile literature
        I. Title II. Glover, Penny
        629.2'275

ISBN: 978 0 7502 6156 2

Printed in China

Wayland is a division of Hachette Children's Books
www.hachette.co.uk

Contents

What are motorbikes?

Motorbikes are vehicles with two wheels and an **engine**. The rider sits on top of the motorbike. Motorbikes are fun to ride. They are smaller than cars and use less **fuel**.

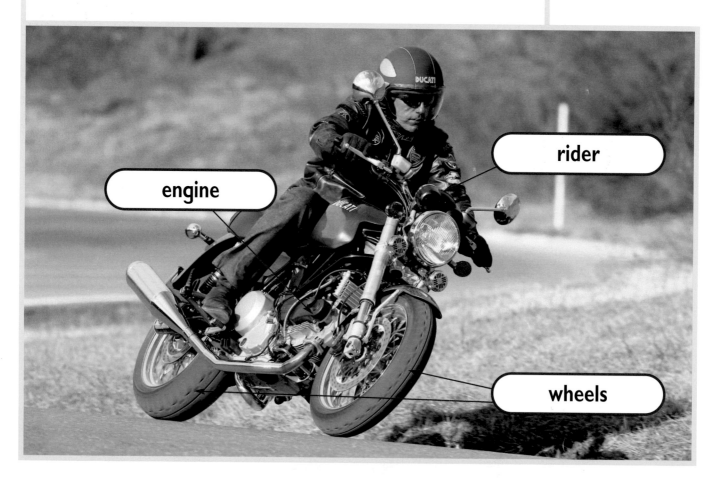

rider

engine

wheels

Motorbikes can travel on roads and tracks. This farmer uses his motorbike to find his sheep in the fields.

sheep

Motorbike quiz
How many wheels does a motorbike have?

Motorbike parts

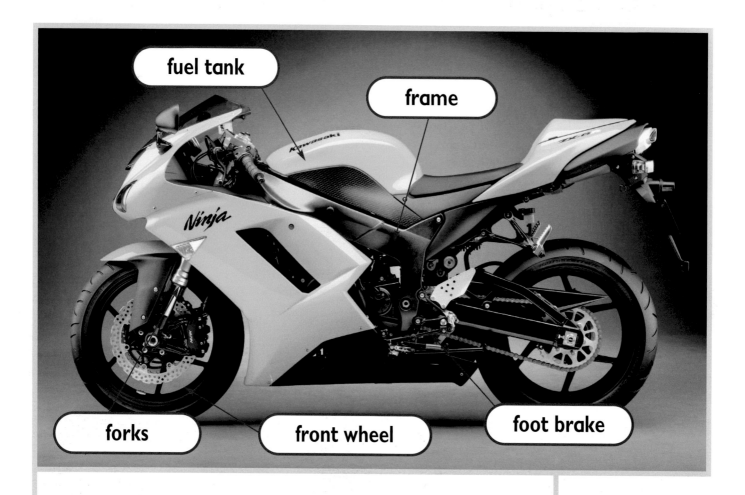

fuel tank

frame

forks

front wheel

foot brake

The motorbike's engine is fixed to a strong **frame**. The rider sits above the engine, behind the fuel tank. The **forks** fix the front wheel to the bike. They turn so the rider can steer the bike.

The rider holds the **handlebars** to control the bike. He turns the **throttle** to speed up, and squeezes the **brake** to slow down. The **speedometer** shows how fast the rider is going.

brakes

handlebars

speedometer

throttle

Motorbike quiz

How does the rider make the bike speed up?

What makes it go?

The engine makes the motorbike go. It needs **petrol** to make it work. The rider fills the tank with petrol at the garage.

The motorbike is like a bicycle but instead of the rider pedalling, the engine does the work.

engine

Motorbike quiz
What does the engine need to make it work?

Police bike

The police bike is powerful and fast. Flashing lights and a loud noise warn people when it is speeding to an emergency. Police officers in the USA ride Harley Davidson motorbikes.

Fire-fighting bike

Some fire-fighters ride motorbikes too. In crowded city streets a fire-fighting bike is faster than a fire truck.

Delivery bike

These bikes deliver pizza. They are quick and easy to park, so the pizza arrives hot!

Motorbike quiz
What make of motorbike do some policemen ride in the USA?

Scooters

mirrors

step-through frame

A **scooter** is a motorbike
with a **step-through frame**.
Scooters are light and easy to ride.
They are good for city travel.

These police officers in Brazil are riding on electric scooters. Electric scooters are quiet and do not make **fumes**.

electric scooter

Motorbike quiz
What kind of frame does a scooter have?

Quad bikes

Quad bikes have four wheels instead of two. A quad bike's thick tyres let it cross soft ground where a motorbike would get stuck. Quad bikes are 'All Terrain Vehicles' or **ATVs**.

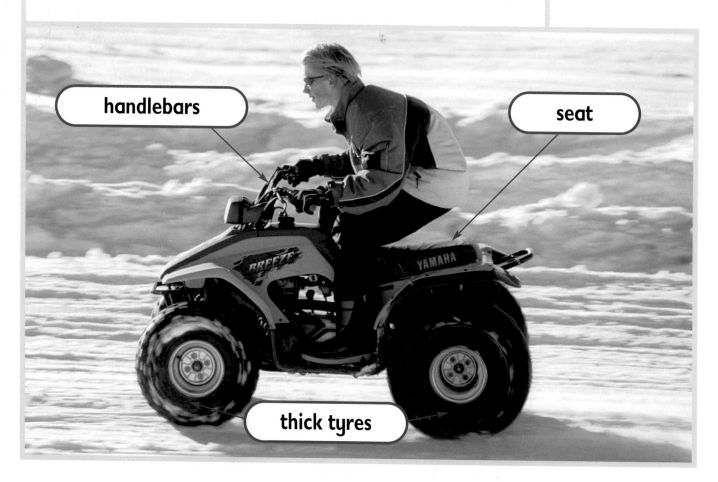

handlebars

seat

thick tyres

A lifeguard uses a quad bike to patrol the beach. The thick tyres are good for driving on sand.

Motorbike quiz
What is an ATV?

Record breakers

Special motorbikes called **Streamliners** are the fastest in the world. They can only go in straight lines.

The Suzuki Hayabusa is the world's fastest road bike. It can reach 200 miles per hour.

This is one of
the smallest bikes
in the world.
It is called the
pocket bike.

Motorbike quiz
What is the fastest
road bike?

Riding safely

Riding a motorbike is more dangerous than driving a car. Riders must always wear **crash helmets** and leather clothes to protect them if they fall off.

crash helmet

leather clothes

Before you can ride a motorbike you must pass a test. New riders learn how to control their motorbikes at a riding school.

Motorbike quiz
What must you do before you can ride a motorbike?

Motorbike fun

Motorbikes take part in races and displays. Grand Prix races are the fastest. The riders lean to the side to speed around the bends.

Motocross races are on rough, bumpy tracks. The motorbikes fly through the air at the tops of hills.

Motorbike display teams do tricks and stunts. The riders must practise to make their stunts safe.

Motorbike quiz
What kind of track do motocross bikes race on?

Old motorbikes

Motorbikes have changed over the years. This is the first motorbike with a petrol engine. It was made more than one hundred years ago. Its top speed was 8 miles per hour.

Motorbike words

ATV
All Terrain Vehicle: a vehicle that can go on any kind of ground, not just smooth roads.

brake
The part of a motorbike that slows it down.

crash helmet
A strong, hard helmet that every motorbike rider must wear to protect their heads.

engine
The part of the motorbike that makes it go.

forks
The parts that fix the front wheel to the frame.

frame
The main part to which all the other parts of the motorbike are fixed.

fuel
Something that burns inside an engine to make it work.

fumes
Dirty clouds of smoke that some engines give out.

handlebars
The part the rider holds and turns to steer the motorbike.

petrol
The fuel most motorbikes use to make them go.

pocket bike
One of the smallest motorbikes.

quad bike
A vehicle like a motorbike but with four wheels.

scooter
A motorbike with a step-through frame.

speedometer
The part that shows the rider how fast the motorbike is going.

step-through frame
The low frame of a scooter that makes it easy to ride.

Streamliner
The fastest bike in the world. It only travels in straight lines.

throttle
The part of a motorbike that speeds it up.

Quiz answers

Page 5 Two.

Page 7 By turning the throttle.

Page 9 Petrol.

Page 11 Harley Davidson.

Page 13 A step-through frame.

Page 15 An All Terrain Vehicle.

Page 17 The Suzuki Hayabusa.

Page 19 Pass a test.

Page 21 Bumpy tracks.

Index